The FIRE WITHIN

D1565224

Ronald Rolheiser

The FIRE WITHIN

*Desire, Sexuality, Longing,
and God*

PARACLETE PRESS
Brewster, Massachusetts

Library of Congress Cataloging-in-Publication Data
Names: Rolheiser, Ronald, author.
Title: The fire within : desire, sexuality, longing, and God / Ronald
  Rolheiser.
Description: Brewster, Massachusetts : Paraclete Press, 2021. | Summary:
  "Christianity has struggled mightily with sex, and so too have most
  other religions, yet when we look at sexual desire and ask where it
  comes from, there can be only one answer: it comes from God"-- Provided
  by publisher.
Identifiers: LCCN 2020044727 (print) | LCCN 2020044728 (ebook) | ISBN
  9781640606661 (tradepaper) | ISBN 9781640606678 (epub) | ISBN
  9781640606685 (pdf)
Subjects: LCSH: Sex--Religious aspects--Christianity. | Desire--Religious
  aspects--Christianity.
Classification: LCC BT708 .R567 2021 (print) | LCC BT708 (ebook) | DDC
  233/.5--dc23
LC record available at https://lccn.loc.gov/2020044727
LC ebook record available at https://lccn.loc.gov/2020044728

10 9 8 7 6 5 4 3 2 1

Published by Paraclete Press
Brewster, Massachusetts
www.paracletepress.com

Printed in the United States of America

CONTENTS

PART ONE
Desire and Our Complex Humanity

PART TWO
Dealing Humanly and Spiritually with Desire

At the age of eighteen, I entered religious life and began what is called novitiate. We were a group of twenty, all of us in our late teens or early twenties, and despite our commitment to religious life we were understandably restless, lonely, and fraught with sexual tension. One day we were given a talk from a visiting priest who began his conference with this question: "Are you guys a little restless? Feeling a bit cooped up here?" We nodded. He went on: "Well, you should be! You must be jumping out of your skins! All that young energy, boiling inside you! You must be going crazy! But it's okay; that's what you should be feeling if you're healthy! It's normal, it's good. You're young; that's what youth feels like!"

Hearing this freed up something inside me. For the first time, in a language that actually spoke to me, someone had given me sacred permission to be at home inside my own skin.

It is normal to feel restless as a child, lonely as a teenager, and frustrated by lack of intimacy as an adult; after all, we live with insatiable desires of every kind, none of which will ever find complete fulfillment this side of eternity.

Where do these desires come from? Why are they so insatiable? What is their meaning?

The Catholic catechisms I was instructed from as a young boy and sermons I heard from the pulpit essentially answered those questions, but in a vocabulary far too abstract, theological, and churchy to do much for me existentially. They left me sensing there was an answer, but not one for me. So, I suffered my loneliness quietly. Moreover, I agonized because I felt that it was somehow not right to feel the way I did. My religious instruction, rich as it was, did not offer any benevolent smile from God on my restlessness and dissatisfaction. Puberty and the conscious stirring of sexuality within me made things worse. Now not only was I restless and dissatisfied, but also the raw feelings and fantasies that were besetting me were considered positively sinful.

That was my state of mind when I entered religious life and the seminary. Of course, the restlessness continued, but eventually my philosophical and theological studies gave me some understanding of what was so relentlessly stirring inside me and gave me sacred permission to be okay with that.

As I look back on my studies, a number of salient persons stand out in helping me understand the wildness, insatiability, meaning, and ultimate goodness of human desire. The first was St. Augustine. The now-famous quote with which he begins his *Confessions*: "You have made us for yourself, Lord, and our hearts are restless until they rest in you," has forever served me as the key to tie everything else together. With that as my key for synthesis, I met this axiom in Thomas Aquinas: "The adequate object of the intellect and will is all being as such." That might sound abstract, but even as a twenty-year-old, I grasped its meaning: in brief, what would you need to experience to finally say, "I am satisfied. Enough!" Aquinas's answer: *Everything*!

Later in my studies, I read Karl Rahner. Like Aquinas, he too can seem hopelessly abstract when, for instance, he defines the human person as "Obediential potency living inside a supernatural existential."[1] Really? Well, what he means by that can be translated into a single counsel he once offered a friend: "In the torment of the insufficiency of everything attainable we ultimately learn that here, in this life, there is no finished symphony."[2]

Finally, in my studies, I met the person and thought of Henri Nouwen. He continued to teach me what it means to live with your own pathological complexity, and he articulated this with a unique genius and in a fresh vocabulary. Reading Nouwen was like being introduced to myself, while still standing inside all my shadows. He helped give me the sense that it is normal, healthy, and not impure or unholy to feel all those wild stirrings with their concomitant temptations inside me.

Desire, restlessness, and sexuality constitute a formidable trinity.

Each of us is a bundle of untamed eros, of wild desire, of longing, of restlessness, of loneliness, of dissatisfaction, of sexuality, and of insatiability. Inside all that disquiet we need two things: an understanding of why (as Pascal once said) we cannot sit still in a room for one hour, and sacred permission to know it is normal and good to feel that way. In short, we need to know that our restlessness makes sense and that God is smiling on it.

One extra note on the particular restlessness we call sexuality. For most religious people, the words *God* and *sex* never go together. God is conceived of as holy, pure, sexless, and as morally above the raw desires that so powerfully beset us. Sex, on the other hand, is conceived of as earthy and unholy, something we must snatch, and not without guilt, from the gods. Christianity has struggled mightily with sex; so too have most other religions. It is hard to look with unblinking eyes at the perceived tension between God and sex. Piety and propriety prohibit it, and it is noteworthy that in the three great religious traditions that ultimately worship the same God, Judaism, Christianity, and Islam, God is conceived of in the popular mind as a male celibate, masculine with no wife. So it is understandably difficult to postulate that sexuality finds its origins in God and even harder to not believe that those powerfully raw and earthy desires we feel are not at odds with what is pure and holy. And yet when we look at sexual desire and ask where it comes from, there can be only one answer. It comes from God. The same is true for its meaning.

Sexuality is inside us to help lure us back to God, bring us into a community of life with each other, and let us take part in God's generativity. If that is true, and it is, then given its origin and meaning, its earthiness notwithstanding, sex does not set us against what is holy and pure. It is a Godly energy.

This is a book on desire, its experience, its origins, its meaning, and how it might be generatively channeled. T. S. Eliot in his masterful poem *Four Quartets* describes love and sin as two kinds of fire, with both saint and sinner feeding off the same divine energy but feeling that fire very differently. We will all be consumed by the fire, by desire; it is only a question of which kind of fire. "We only live, only suspire," Eliot writes, "consumed by either fire or fire."[3] One brings peace, the other torment.

Dealing with this fire inside us is a lifelong struggle. As Gabriel Marcel might say, this is a mystery to be lived, not a problem to be solved. Trying to shed light on that mystery and the journey it takes us on has been perhaps the principal motif underlying my writing throughout more than forty years. What is offered here is not an attempt at some comprehensive vision—I have attempted that in other books[4]—but, rather, some tantalizing fragments that can help give us permission to feel what we feel and know that God is still smiling on us.

Ronald Rolheiser
January 2, 2021

PART ONE

Desire and Our Complex Humanity

CHAPTER 1

LONGING AT THE CENTER OF OUR EXPERIENCE

At the core of experience, at the center of our hearts, there is longing. At every level, our being aches and we are full of tension. We give different names to it—loneliness, restlessness, emptiness, longing, yearning, nostalgia, wanderlust, inconsummation. To be a human being is to be fundamentally dis-eased.

And this dis-ease lies at the center of our lives, not at the edges. We are not fulfilled persons who occasionally get lonely, restful people who sometimes experience restlessness, or persons who live in habitual intimacy and have episodic battles with alienation and inconsummation. The reverse is truer. We are lonely people who occasionally experience fulfillment, restless souls who sometimes feel restful, and aching hearts that have brief moments of consummation.

Longing and yearning are so close to the core of the human person that some theologians define loneliness as being the human soul; that is, the human soul is not something that gets lonely, it is a loneliness. The soul is not something that has a cavity of loneliness within it; it is a cavity of loneliness, a Grand Canyon without a bottom, a cavern of longing created by God. The cavern is not something in the soul. It is the soul. The soul is not a something that has a capacity for God. It is a capacity for God.

When Augustine says, "You have made us for yourself, Lord, and our hearts are restless until they rest in you," he is, of course, pointing out the reason why God would have made us this way. And, as his prayer indicates, the ultimate value of longing lies precisely in its incessant nature; by never letting us rest with anything less than the infinite and eternal, it guarantees that we will seek God or be frustrated.

But beyond its ultimate purpose, to direct us toward our final purpose, the experience of longing has another central task in the soul. Metaphorically, it is the heat that forges the soul. The pain of longing is a fire that shapes us inside. How? What does the pain of longing do to the soul? What is the value in living in a certain perpetual frustration? What is gained by carrying tension?

Superficially, and this argument has been written up many times, carrying tension helps us appreciate the consummation when it finally comes. Thus, temporary frustration makes eventual fulfillment so much sweeter, hunger makes food taste better, and only after sublimation can there be anything sublime. There is a lot of truth in that. But the pain of loneliness and longing shapes the soul too in other, more important, ways. All great literature takes its root precisely in this: how carrying tension shapes a soul.

Longing shapes the soul in many ways, particularly by helping create the space within us where God can be born. Longing creates in us the stable and the manger of Bethlehem. It is the trough into which God can be born.

This is an ancient idea. Already centuries before Christ, Jewish apocalyptic literature had the motif: Every tear brings the Messiah closer. Taken literally, this might sound like bad theology—a certain quota of pain must be endured before God can come—but it is a beautiful, poetic expression of very sound theology: carrying tension stretches, expands, and swells the heart, creating in it the space within which God can come. Carrying tension is what the Bible means by "pondering."

Pierre Teilhard de Chardin left us a great image for this. For him, the soul, just like the body, has a temperature, and for Teilhard, what longing does is to raise the temperature of the soul. Longing, restlessness, yearning, and carrying tension raise our psychic temperatures. This, a raised temperature, has a number of effects on the soul.

First, analogous to what happens in physical chemistry, where unions that cannot take place at lower temperatures will often take place at higher ones, longing and yearning open us to unions that otherwise would not happen, particularly in terms of our relationship to God and the things of heaven, though the idea is not without its value within the realm of human intimacy. Put more simply, in our loneliness we sizzle and eventually burn away a lot of the coldness and other obstacles that block union.

Moreover, this sizzling longing brings the Messiah closer because it swells the heart so that it becomes more what God created it to be—a Grand Canyon, without a bottom, that aches in lonely inconsummation until it finds its resting place in God.

CHAPTER 2

RAW DESIRE

There are certain times in life when blind, relentless desire makes itself shamelessly evident, in a baby and in an adolescent.

We see blind desire in a baby. An infant takes everything to its mouth indiscriminately, shamelessly, without any sense of control, of good or bad, or of morality, propriety, or consequence. A baby simply blindly reaches out for gratification and tries to drink it in. There is considerable danger in that. Babies often hurt themselves.

We see somewhat of the same thing in the adolescent. At puberty, the body shoots huge doses of hormones into the adolescent and a period of blind, obsessive restlessness follows. There is a crass, oftentimes shameless, reaching out and, as in the baby, this blind desire makes for a dangerous period. Adolescents also frequently hurt themselves, not to mention others, while in the grip of this energy.

When desire is blind, inchoate, and uninitiated, as in the baby or adolescent, it is dangerous—both for the person who has it and for those who are nearby. But this desire is also, as we shall soon suggest, the energy that lies at the very center of life. It is a divine energy. As such, it should not be repressed, ignored, shamed, or put down. Neither should it be given free scope to act out. It should be honored and disciplined through a proper initiation process.

How do you honor and channel blind desire in a child? By accepting that energy for what it is, the deep principle of life made manifest. Accordingly, we should never shame it: "You are a pig!" "You are selfish!" The child should never be made to feel dirty and guilty for having this energy. Instead the child should be initiated into its fuller meaning by connecting this desire to the heart of life itself within the family. This sounds abstract, but what it means is that we take this raw energy within the child, the desire to eat, and discipline it by connecting it to the much deeper joy of dining, of sharing food, life, and love within a family and community. There is a discipline in that. The child has to learn boundaries, respect, and manners, but discipline, controlling the desire, is not the ultimate goal. The goal is taking that raw desire and linking its energy to the center of community life.

If we can do that, we will produce a healthy child, namely, one who is able to discipline its appetite and yet thoroughly enjoy, without guilt, the pleasures of eating.

It is this principle that we must use to initiate adolescents at that other raw moment of life, the onset of puberty. At that moment, just as in infancy, raw desire is rampantly manifest, not just in terms of sex but also in terms of grandiosity. In the adolescent, desire is, again, raw, wild, and dangerous.

What's to be done? As in the child, that energy needs both to be honored and disciplined. Just as in the child, this is done by connecting her or him to what lies at the heart of the community.

Thus, raw desire—sex, grandiose dreams—within the teenager is not to be belittled or shamed. It needs to be honored. You don't tell a teenager struggling with this: "You are an animal!" "You are an unrealistic dreamer!" Just as in the child, one does not discipline raw energy by making the person feel guilty, dirty, or worthless. This energy, irrespective of its crass manifestations, is sacred. It is the pulse of life itself flowing through us, part of God's creative energy incarnate in our bodies, the groaning of the Holy Spirit, deeper than words, praying through us. It is spirit seeking connection.

To paraphrase Michael Meade: Within youth, nature sets loose a series of eruptions.[5] The youth heats up biologically and emotionally and is seared from the inside. The youth is driven to seek an outer experience that will match that inner heat and turmoil. If he or she doesn't get connected to the warmth and beauty at the heart of the community, he or she will burn and rage with injustice, or turn cold with resentment and depression.

We do not help, nor discipline, our young people by making them feel guilty about sex or grandiosity. We must honor that energy in them but connect it to the heart of life in such a way that, feeling its sacredness and life-giving energy, they become infinitely more reverent before its great power.

CHAPTER 3

FEEDING OFF SACRED FIRE

See the wise and wicked ones /
Who feed upon life's sacred fire . . .

These are lines from Gordon Lightfoot's song "Don Quixote,"[6] and they highlight an important truth: both the wise and the wicked feed off the same energy. And it's good energy, sacred energy, divine energy, irrespective of its use. The greedy and the violent feed off the same energy as do the wise and the saints. There's one source of energy, and, even though it can be irresponsibly, selfishly, and horrifically misused, it remains always God's energy.

Unfortunately, we don't often think of things that way. Recently I was listening to a very discouraged man who, looking at the selfishness, greed, and violence in our world, blamed it all on the devil. "It must be the anti-Christ," he said. "How else do you explain all this, so many people breaking basically every commandment."

He's right in his assessment that the selfishness, greed, and violence we see in our world today are anti-Christ (though perhaps not the Anti-Christ spoken of in Scripture). However, he's wrong about where selfishness, greed, and violence are drawing their energy from. The energy they are drawing upon comes from God, not from the devil. What we see in all the negative things that make up so much of the evening news each day is not evil energy but rather the misuse of sacred energy. Evil deeds are not the result of evil energies but the result of the misuse of sacred energy. Whether you consider the devil a person or a metaphor, either way, he has no other origin than from God. God created the devil and created him good. His wickedness results from the misuse of that goodness.

All energy comes from God and all energy is good, but it can be wickedly misused. Moreover, it's ironic that the ones who seem to drink most deeply from the wellsprings of divine energy are, invariably, the best and the worst, the wise and the wicked, saints and sinners. These mainline the fire. The rest of us, living in the gap between saints and sinners, tend to struggle more to actually catch fire, to truly drink deeply from the wellsprings of divine energy. Our struggle isn't so much in misusing divine energy, but rather in not succumbing to chronic numbness, depression, fatigue, flatness, bitterness, envy, and the kind of discouragement that has us going through life lacking fire and forever protesting that we have a right to be uncreative and unhappy. Great saints and great sinners don't live lives of "quiet desperation," to quote Henry David Thoreau; they drink deeply sacred energy, become inflamed by that fire, and make that the source for either their extraordinary wisdom or their wild wickedness.

This insight—saints and sinners feed off the same source—isn't just an interesting irony. It's an important truth that can help us better understand our relationship to God, to the things of this world, and to ourselves. We must be clear on what's good and what's bad, otherwise we end up both misunderstanding ourselves and misunderstanding the energies of our world.

A healthy spirituality needs to be predicated on a proper understanding of God, ourselves, the world, and the energies that drive our world, and these are the non-negotiable Christian principles within which we need to understand ourselves, the world, and the use of our energies: First, God is good, God is the source of all energy everywhere, and that energy is good. Second, we are made by God, we are good, and our nature is not evil. Finally, everything in our world has been made by God and it too is good.

So where do sin and evil enter? They enter in when we misuse the good energy that God has given us, and they enter in when we relate in bad ways to the good things of creation. Simply put: We are good and creation around us is good, but we can relate to it in the wrong way, precisely through selfishness, greed, or violence. Likewise, our energies are good, including all those energies that underlie our propensity toward pride, greed, lust, envy, anger, and sloth. But we can misuse those energies and draw upon life's sacred fire in very self-serving, lustful, greedy, and wicked ways.

Sin and evil, therefore, arise out of the misuse of our energies, not out of the energies themselves. So, too, sin and evil arise out of how we relate to certain things in the world, not out of some inherent evil inside of our own persons or inside of the things themselves. The wicked aren't evil persons drawing energy from the devil. They're good people, irresponsibly and selfishly misusing sacred energy. The energy itself is still good, despite its misuse.

We don't tap into evil energies when we give in to greed, lust, envy, sloth, or anger. No, rather we misuse the good and sacred energy within which we live and move and have our being. The wise and wicked both feed off the same sacred fire.[7]

CHAPTER 4

CAVERNS OF FEELING

There is a story in the Old Testament that both shocks and fascinates by its sheer earthiness. It's found in Judges, chapter 11.

A certain king, Jephthah, is at war, and things are going badly for him and his army. In desperation he prays to God, promising that if he is granted victory he will, upon returning home, offer in sacrifice the first person he meets. His prayer is heard, and he is given victory. When he returns home, he is horrified, because the first person he meets, whom he must now kill in sacrifice, is his only daughter, in the full bloom of her youth, whom he loves most dearly. He tells his daughter of his promise and offers to break it rather than sacrifice her. She, however, insists that he go through with his promise, but there is one condition: She needs, before she dies, time in the desert to bewail the fact that she is to die a virgin, incomplete, unconsummated. She asks her father for two months' time during which she goes into the desert with her maiden companions and mourns her unfulfilled life. Afterward she returns and offers herself in sacrifice.

Despite the unfortunate patriarchal character of this story, it is a parable that in its own earthy way says something quite profound, namely, that we must mourn what's incomplete and unconsummated within our lives.

In the end, we all die, as did Jephthah's daughter, as virgins, our lives incomplete, our deepest dreams and deepest yearnings largely frustrated, still looking for intimacy, unconsciously bewailing our virginity. This is true of married people just as it is true for celibates. Ultimately, we all sleep alone.

And this must be mourned. Whatever form this might take, each of us must, at some point, go into the desert and bewail our virginity—mourn the fact that we will die unfulfilled, incomplete. It's when we fail to do this—and because we fail to do it—that we go through life being too demanding, too angry, too bitter, too disappointed, and too prone to constantly blame others and life itself for our frustrations. When we fail to mourn properly our incomplete lives, then this incompleteness becomes a haunting depression, an unyielding restlessness, and a bitter center that robs our lives of all delight.

It is because we do not mourn our virginity that we demand that someone or something—a marriage partner, a sexual partner, an ideal family, having children, an achievement, a vocational goal, or a job—take all of our loneliness away. That, of course, is an unreal expectation that invariably leads to bitterness and disappointment. In this life there is no completeness. We are built for the infinite. Our hearts, minds, and souls are Grand Canyons without a bottom. Because of that we will, this side of eternity, always be lonely, restless, incomplete, still a virgin—living in the torment of the insufficiency of everything attainable.

My parents' generation tended to recognize this more easily than we do. They prayed, daily, the prayer, "To thee do we send up our sighs, mourning and weeping in this valley of tears." That prayer, and others like them, were their way of bewailing their virginity.

Contemporary spirituality tends to reject such an emphasis on the limitations of this life as unhealthy and a bit morbid. That is arguable. What is not is the fact that we never, here in this life, find the panacea to our loneliness. Any balanced, truly life-giving spirituality must take this into account and challenge people to understand, integrate, and live out that fact. Perhaps the best way to do this is not the way of my parents' generation, who sometimes put more emphasis on life after death than upon life after birth. Maybe it is a bit morbid to consider this life so much a "vale of tears." But tears must be factored in. Otherwise, in the end, we are falsely challenged, and the symbolic infrastructure of our spirituality is inadequate to handle our actual experience.

The daydreams of our childhood eventually die, but the source that ultimately fires them, our infinite caverns of feeling, do not. We ache just as much, even after we know the daydream can never, this side of eternity, come true. Hence, like Jephthah's daughter, we must come to a time when we go into the desert and mourn the fact that we are to die a virgin.

CHAPTER 5

OUR CONGENITAL COMPLEXITY

The renowned spiritual writer Ruth Burrows begins her autobiography with these words: "I was born into this world with a tortured sensitivity. For long I have puzzled over the causes of my psychological anguish."[8]

Unfortunately, to our loss, too many spiritual biographies don't begin like this, that is, by recognizing right at the start the bewildering, pathological complexity inside our own nature. We're not simple in heart, mind, and soul, nor indeed even in body. Each of us has enough complexity within us to write our own treatise on abnormal psychology.

And that complexity must not only be recognized, it needs to be respected and hallowed because it stems not from what's worst in us but from what's best in us. We're complex because what beguiles us inside and tempts us in every direction is not, first of all, the wiliness of the devil but rather the image and likeness of God. Inside us there's a divine fire, a greatness, that gives us infinite depth, insatiable desires, and enough luminosity to bewilder every psychologist. The image and likeness of God inside us, as John of the Cross writes, renders our hearts, minds, and souls "caverns" too deep to ever be filled in or fully understood.

It's my belief that Christian spirituality, at least in its popular preaching and catechesis, has too often not taken this seriously enough. In short, the impression has too much been given that Christian discipleship shouldn't be complicated: Why all this resistance within you! What's wrong with you! But, as we know from our own experience, our innate complexity is forever throwing up complications and resistances to becoming a saint, to "willing the one thing." Moreover, because our complexity hasn't been recognized and honored spiritually, we often feel guilty about it. Why am I so complicated? Why do I have all these questions? Why am I so often confused? Why is sex such a powerful impulse? Why do I have so many temptations?

The simple answer is, because we are born with a godly fire within. Thus, the source of so many of our confusions, temptations, and resistances comes as much from what best in us as from the wiles of Satan and the world.

What should we do in the face of our own bewildering complexity? Here are some counsels for the long haul:

* *Honor and hallow your complexity.* Accept that this is a God-given gift inside you and, at the end of the day, it's what is best inside you. It's what separates you from plants and animals. Their nature is simple, but having an immortal, infinite soul makes

for lots of complications as you struggle to live out your life within the finitude that besets you.

* *Never underestimate your complexity—even as you resist massaging it.* Recognize and respect the "demons and angels" that roam freely inside your heart and mind. But don't massage your complexity either, by fancying yourself as the tormented artist or as the existentialist who's heroically out of step with life.

* *Befriend your shadow.* It's the luminosity you've split off. Slowly, with proper caution and support, begin to face the inner things that frighten you.

* *Hallow the power and place of sexuality within you.* You're incurably sexual, and for a godly reason. Never deny or denigrate the power of sexuality— even as you carry it with a proper chastity.

* *Name your wounds, grieve them, mourn your inconsummation.* Whatever wounds that you don't grieve will eventually snakebite you. Accept and mourn the fact that here, in this life, there is no completeness.

* *Never let the "transcendental impulse" inside you become drugged or imprisoned.* Your complexity continually lets you know that you're built for more than this life. Never deaden this impulse inside you. Learn to recognize, through your frustrations and fantasies, the ways you often imprison it.

* *Try to find a "higher love" by which to transcend the more immediate power of your natural instincts.* All miracles begin with falling in love. Hallow your spontaneous impulses and temptations by searching for that higher love and higher value toward which they're pointing. Offering others your altruism and the gaze of admiration will feel so good and right that it will bring to fulfillment what you're really yearning for.

* *Let your own complexity teach you understanding and empathy.* By being in touch with your own complexity you will eventually learn that nothing is foreign to you and that what you see on the newscasts each day mirrors what's inside you.

* *Forgive yourself often.* Your complexity will trip you up many times, and so you will need to forgive yourself many times. Live, knowing that God's mercy is a well that's never exhausted.

* *Live under God's patience and understanding.* God is your builder, the architect who constructed you and who is responsible for your complexity. Trust that God understands. Trust that God is more anxious about you than you're anxious about yourself. The God who knows all things also knows and appreciates why you struggle.

CHAPTER 6

OUR STRUGGLE WITH GRANDIOSITY

We wake up into life with the incurable sense that we're special, that we're the center of the universe. And, subjectively, we are! In our awareness, we're the center of the universe and life does revolve around us. Our own being is what's most massively real to us. As Descartes famously said, the only thing that we know for sure is real is our own selves; *I think, therefore, I am.* We may be dreaming everything else.

Spirituality has perennially judged this negatively. Egocentricity, feelings of grandiosity, self-centeredness, and pride were seen as the result of the corruption of human nature through original sin. We called it The Fall. Our first parents attempted to overreach, to be more than God intended them to be, and this irrevocably corrupted their nature—and we, their children, inherit this. So we, adult children of Adam and Eve, too instinctually tend to overreach, to puff up in self-importance, to fill with pride, and think first about ourselves.

That doctrine of original sin has something important to say, but it isn't first of all to shame us in our natural pride and sense of specialness. The real reason why pride and grandiosity are incurably ingrained inside us is because God built us that way, and that, of itself, is not a fault or a corruption but instead constitutes what's highest and most precious inside us. Both Christianity and Judaism take as dogma that we're born, every one of us, in the image and likeness of God. That's not to be imagined piously as some beautiful icon stamped inside our souls but rather as fire, divine fire, which because it is godly brings with it a sense of the preciousness, dignity, and uniqueness of our lives. But with that too come (as part of the same package) pride and grandiosity. Simply put, we can't have Godliness inside us and not feel ourselves as special.

And that makes for a less-than-serene situation for the planet. We're now eight billion people on this earth, each one with the same innate sense that he or she is the center of the universe and that his or her own reality is what's most real. That's the real cause behind what you see happening on the world news each night, for worse and for better. Grandiosity is the source of human strife, but equally the source of human greatness.

Important in our understanding of this is that our innate sense of godliness is also the place where we suffer our deepest wounds. What most wounds the image and likeness of God inside us? These things: humiliation, lack of adequate self-expression, the perennial frustration of bumping up against the limits of life, and the martyrdom of obscurity.

Each of us, by our nature, possesses a divinely given uniqueness and dignity, and thus nothing wounds us more than being humiliated and shamed in our struggle to live this out. A shameful humiliation, even as a very young child, can scar us for the rest of our lives. It's one of the reasons why we have mass killings. Likewise, as the novelist Iris Murdoch once said, the greatest human pain is the pain of inadequate self-expression. There's a great artist, composer, teacher, athlete, and performer inside each of us, but few people can ever give that satisfying expression. The rest of us have to live with perennial frustration because what's deepest in us lies unexpressed. We're forever bumping up against the real limits of our own lives and the limits of life itself. In the end, all of us die with a life that was never fully consummated. And that isn't easily accepted! Everything inside us militates against this. Finally, almost all of us live a certain martyrdom of obscurity, recognized and famous only inside our own daydreams, our greatness hidden from the world. That too isn't easily accepted.

What's to be taken away from this? Since we secretly nurse thoughts of specialness should we also nurse a secret shame? Is our innate pride something that sets us against holiness? Is our grandiosity a bad thing? Is our frustration with the limits and inadequacy of our lives something that displeases God? Are our daydreams of uniqueness and greatness something that taints our contemplation and prayer? Is our nature, of itself, somehow corrupt? Must we somehow step outside of our own skin to be saints?

Each of these questions can be answered in two ways. Grandiosity, pride, shame, frustration, and daydreams of greatness can indeed be our downfall and turn us into awful persons, selfish, jealous, spiteful, and murderous. But they can also be the source of greatness, of nobility of soul, of generosity, of selflessness, of generativity, of true prayer, and can turn us into selfless martyrs of faith, hope, and charity. Our godliness is a very mixed blessing; but it is, no doubt, our greatest blessing.

CHAPTER 7

INCHOATE DESIRE

Sometimes while praying the Psalms I'm caught looking quite uncomfortably into a mirror reflecting back at me my own seeming dishonesty. For example, we pray these words from the Psalms: "My soul longs for you. . . . As the deer longs for streams of water, so my soul longs for you, O God (42:1, 2)." "For you my body yearns; for you my soul thirsts"! (63:2).

If I'm honest, I have to admit that a lot of times, perhaps most times, my soul longs for a lot of things that do not seem of God. How often can I honestly pray, *For you, God, alone do I long. For you alone do I thirst!* In my restlessness, earthy desires, and natural instincts, I long for many things that don't appear very God-focused or heavenly at all. I suspect that's true for most of us for good parts of our lives. Rare is the mystic who can say those prayers and mean them with her full heart on any given day.

But human desire is a complex thing. There's a surface and there's a depth, and in every one of our longings and motivations we can ask ourselves this: What am I really looking for here? I know what I want on the surface, here and now, but what am I ultimately longing for in this?

This discrepancy, between what we're aware of on the surface and what's sensed only in some dark, inchoate way at a deeper level, is what's captured in a distinction that philosophers make between what's *explicit* in our awareness and what's *implicit* within it. The explicit refers to what we are aware of consciously ("I want this particular thing"); whereas the implicit refers to the unconscious factors that are also in play but of which we are unaware. These we only sense, vaguely, in some unconscious part of our soul.

For instance, Karl Rahner, who was fond of this distinction and who puts it to good use in his spirituality, offers us this (crass though clear) example of the distinction between the explicit and the implicit within our motivation and desires. Imagine this, he says: A man, lonely and restless and depressed on a Saturday night, goes to a singles' bar, picks up a prostitute, and goes to bed with her. On the surface his motivation and desire are as undisguised as they are crass. He's not longing for God in his bed on this particular night. Or is he?

On the surface, of course he's not; his desire seems purely self-centered and the antithesis of holy longing. But, parsed out to its deepest root, his desire is ultimately a longing for divine intimacy, for the bread of life, for heaven. He's longing for God at the very depth of his soul and at the very depth of his motivation, except he isn't aware of this. Raw desire for immediate gratification is all that he's consciously aware of at this time, but this doesn't change his ultimate motivation, of which this is a symptom. At a deeper level, of which he is not consciously aware, he's still longing for the bread of life, for God alone. His soul is still that of a deer, longing for clear, flowing streams, except that on this given night another stream is promising him a more immediate tonic that he can have right now.

Long ago, now, I taught a course on the spirituality of aging and dying. Stealing a line from Goethe's poem "Holy Longing," I entitled the course poetically, "Insane for the Light." In a term paper, one of the students, a woman, reflecting on her own journey toward aging and dying, wrote these words:

> And then last night I began to think that dying is making love with God, the consummation after a lifetime of flirtations, encounters, meetings in the dark, and constant yearning, longing, and sense of loneliness that does make one insane for the light. I reflected on the *Song of Songs* and thought that it could be an analogy of how I see dying, not necessarily as the body's disintegration and demise, but rather as the entire transition that I was born destined to make. I think of my life as a love story with its ups and downs like any love story, but always going in the direction of God with the finality

of death being the wedding of the love between God and myself after a lifetime betrothal.

She puts it as well as Rahner and the philosophers, though her words are more direct. She too, in analyzing her desire, points out there are levels, explicit and implicit, conscious and unconscious.

Yes, our lives, with all their tensions, restlessness, youthful immaturities, adult depressions, cold lonely seasons, times of doubt, times of desperation, breakdowns, and occasional irresponsible exuberance will surely be marked by flirtations and encounters that seem to exhibit desires that are not for the bread of life. But they are, ultimately, and one day they will find and know their full consummation.

CHAPTER 8

UNFINISHED SYMPHONIES

Not long ago, I watched on television a discussion between a prominent religious commentator and several reputable theologians representing various Christian denominations. The commentator hosting the show had asked the theologians the question: "Should it make any difference in the way a Christian lives, whether they believe in life after death?" All the theologians on the panel and the host himself agreed that it should not. They all asserted that, whether or not there is life after death, it should make no difference whatsoever in how a Christian lives their life.

They went further. Explicitly or by insinuation, each suggested that a positive belief in life after death might even be harmful as it could falsely focus a person so much on life after death that he or she never quite gets around to living life after birth. They felt that people who do believe in life after death tend, in a rather childish way, to let a system of promised rewards and threatened punishments affect their behavior as opposed to living out of a more mature moral inner-directedness. Moreover, they suggested that belief in life after death tends to deflect people from deep involvement in the world. Those who believe in a life beyond this one end up being otherworldly in an unhealthy sense.

For all of them, then, the question of life after death was not an important religious and Christian question. They left the viewer with the impression that to think otherwise, to have any preoccupations whatever with thoughts of life after death, is a sign of an immature faith.

There is a certain commendable stoicism in that kind of an attitude but, in the end, it masks a belief that, beyond being religiously false, wreaks much havoc in actual life. Simply put, when we stop believing in life after death there is a very real tendency to demand that this life, here and now, give us something it cannot give, namely, full consummation.

Karl Rahner used to say that we will be haunted and driven by restlessness until we accept the fact that here all symphonies remain unfinished. Our age would do well to listen to him because we demand too much from life. We demand the finished symphony.

We enter this world with mind and heart built for the infinite, with tortured complexity, and with deep insatiable congenital longings. We ache for a great love, to embrace the whole world and everyone in it. There is, as the author of Ecclesiastes puts it, a certain timelessness inside our hearts that puts us out of sync with full peace. We are built for the infinite, but what we meet in life is always the finite. We ache to achieve the perfect, in love and in art, but what we achieve is always limited and blemished. We ache for the eternal but we are frustrated in time.

It is no wonder that we are so demanding . . . in our relationships, our jobs, our vacations, and life in general. It is hard to make a full peace with our own very real limits, of body, mind, and achievement. In all of our lives, there is a huge gap between what our hearts demand and what we can actually attain in this life.

When one does not believe in life after death there is the very real temptation to demand that this life lead us to the finish. After all, we only live once and what a tragedy it would be to go through that one life unfulfilled!

In the parable of the conscientious steward, Jesus points out how the steward who does not expect his master's return sets about beating his fellow servants and eating and drinking with drunkards. The images of violence that Jesus inserts here are metaphors precisely of the type of violence we do to life when we demand that it give us everything.

Conversely, the person who awaits the master's return, who does believe this life is not all, can live in greater patience with the frustrations of a life that refuses to provide us the comfort and answers we desire. When this life is not all, then it is easier to not demand all from it.

PART TWO

Dealing Humanly and Spiritually
with Desire

CHAPTER 9

PERPETUALLY DISTRACTED

There's a story in the Hindu tradition that runs something like this: God and a man are walking down a road. The man asks God: "What is the world like?" God answers: "I'd like to tell you, but my throat is parched. I need a cup of cold water. If you can go and get me a cup of cold water, I'll tell you what the world is like." The man heads off to the nearest house to ask for a cup of cold water. He knocks on the door and it is opened by a beautiful young woman. He asks for a cup of cold water. She answers: "I will gladly get it for you, but it's just time for the noon meal—why don't you come in first and eat." He does.

Thirty years later, they've had five children, he's a respected merchant, she's a respected member of the community. They're in their house one evening when a hurricane comes and uproots their house. The man cries out: "Help me, God!" And a voice comes from the center of the hurricane and says: "Where's my cup of cold water?"

This story is not so much a spiritual criticism as it is a fundamental lesson in anthropology and spirituality: To be a human being is to be perpetually distracted. We aren't persons who live in habitual spiritual awareness who occasionally get distracted. We're persons who live in habitual distraction who occasionally become spiritually aware. We tend be so preoccupied with the ordinary business of living that it takes a hurricane of some sort for God to break through.

C. S. Lewis, commenting on why we tend to turn to God only during a hurricane, once remarked that God is always speaking to us, but normally we aren't aware, aren't listening. Accordingly, pain is God's microphone to a deaf world.[9]

However, none of us want that kind of pain; none of us want some disaster, some health breakdown, or some hurricane to shake us up. We prefer a powerful positive event, a miracle or mini-miracle, to happen to us to awaken God's presence in us because we nurse the false daydream that, if God broke into our lives in some miraculous way, we would then move beyond our distracted spiritual state and get more serious about our spiritual lives. But that's the exact delusion inside the biblical character in the parable of Lazarus and Dives (Luke, chapter 16), where the rich man asks Abraham to send him back from the dead to warn his brothers that they must change their way of living or risk the fiery flames. His plea expresses exactly that false assumption: "If someone comes back from the dead, they will listen to him!" Abraham doesn't buy the logic. He answers: "They have Moses and the Prophets. If they don't listen to them, they won't be convinced either, even if someone comes back from the dead." What lies unspoken but critically important in that reply, something easily missed by us, the readers, is that Jesus has already come back from the dead and we aren't listening to him. Why should we suppose that we would listen to anyone else who comes back from the dead? Our preoccupation with the ordinary business of our lives is so strong that we are not attentive to the one who has already come back from the dead.

Given this truth, the Hindu tale just recounted is, in a way, more consoling than chiding. To be human is to be habitually distracted from spiritual things. Such is human nature. Such is our nature. But knowing that our endless proclivity for distraction is normal doesn't give us permission to be comfortable with that fact. Great spiritual mentors, not the least Jesus, strongly urge us to wake up, to move beyond our over-preoccupation with the affairs of everyday life. Jesus challenges us to not be anxious about how we are to provide for ourselves. He also challenges us to read the signs of the times, namely to see the finger of God, the spiritual dimension of things, in the everyday events of our lives. All great spiritual literature does the same. Today there is a rich literature in most spiritual traditions challenging us to mindfulness, to not be mindlessly absorbed in the everyday affairs of our lives.

But great spiritual literature also assures us that God understands us, that grace respects nature, that God didn't make a mistake in designing human nature, and that God didn't make us in such a way that we find ourselves congenitally distracted and then facing God's anger because we are following our nature. Human nature naturally finds itself absorbed in the affairs of everyday life, and God designed human nature in just this way.

And so, I think, God must be akin to a loving parent or grandparent, looking at his or her children at the family gathering, happy that they have interesting lives that so absorb them, content not to be always the center of their conscious attention.

CHAPTER 10

SEX AS SACRAMENT

A Catholic journalist recently commented that the world will begin to take the church seriously when it talks about sex if the church, first of all, affirms what it should always be affirming, namely, that for married persons the marriage bed is their daily Eucharist.

Sex as a sacrament. Sex as Eucharist. Is this high spiritual truth or is it blasphemy? It can be either, since, within a Christian understanding, sex is precisely either sacrament or perversity.

I remember well an article in the ecumenical journal *Grail*, in which the late British psychiatrist and Catholic theologian Jack Dominian discussed the sacramental role of sex within a marriage. Without denying what traditional Christian thought has always affirmed, that is, that procreation is a function of married sexuality, he goes on to suggest five possibilities (ultimately, sacramental possibilities) that can be realized each time a married couple make love.

First, each time they do make love they, potentially, verify their personal significance to each other. More simply put, each act of sexual intercourse is a reminder of (and a celebration of) the fact that they are the most important person in each other's life. Sexual intercourse, within its proper context, love consecrated through marriage, verifies and celebrates (physically, emotionally, and spiritually) what was pronounced in their marriage vows, namely, "My love is now consecrated, displaced, for you!"

Dietrich Bonhoeffer once told a couple he was marrying: "Today you are young and very much in love. You think that your love will sustain your marriage. Well, I give you the opposite advice: let your marriage sustain your love." Sexual orgasm facilitates a personal encounter that speaks of and demands precisely the type of exclusiveness and fidelity that the marriage vows promise.

Secondly, sexual intercourse is one of the most powerful acts through which a couple reinforce each other's sexual identity, making, as Dominian put it, the woman feel fully feminine and the man fully masculine.

Third, sexual intercourse can be, potentially, a most powerful act of reconciliation, healing, and forgiveness. In all relationships, perhaps especially in married ones, wounds will appear (arising from, among other things, different temperaments, disappointment with each other, past histories, weaknesses and inadequacies) which will, at one level, appear to create an unbridgeable chasm. Sexual orgasm can facilitate a peak experience within which harmony is restored beyond the hurt, not because the hurt is taken away, but because in that peak experience something is felt which, for a second at least, lets persons drop the load of hurt, disappointment, and bitterness and meet in a super reconciliation that is a foretaste of the reconciliation of heaven itself.

Fourth, sexual intercourse is perhaps, singularly, the most powerful way a couple has of telling each other that they wish to continue in this consecrated relationship. Freud once said we understand the structure of a thing by looking at it when it's broken. Thus, we see that within a marriage when the sexual bond is broken, when there is an unwillingness or a hesitancy to sleep with each other, there is, at some level, also some unwillingness or hesitancy to continue the relationship at a very deep level.

Finally, sexual intercourse is, as Dominian so aptly put it, a rich vein of thanksgiving. Orgasm, within a proper relationship, spawns gratitude. Given these possibilities for sex, it does not strain the imagination to see that the marriage bed is, potentially, a sacrament, a daily Eucharist.

A sacrament is, as theology has always said in one fashion or another, someone or something which visibly prolongs a saving action of Christ; it is something visible, fleshy, tangible, incarnate, that somehow makes God present.

More specifically still, what takes place in the marriage bed (between a couple who are properly loving each other) parallels what takes place between ourselves and Christ in the Eucharist. Each Eucharist also has those five possibilities: In that encounter we say to Christ and Christ says to us: "My life is consecrated, displaced, for you." Through that encounter, as well, we reinforce our identity as Christians, are embraced in a super-reconciliation, announce through word and action that we want to continue in a deep relationship with Christ, and are imbued with and express gratitude.

The marriage bed, like the Eucharist, is fleshy, tangible, visible and incarnate. (Not at all a sacrament for angels!) Like the Eucharist too it expresses special love, fidelity, reconciliation, and gratitude in an earthy way. That quality, its earthiness, makes it, like the Eucharist, a very powerful and privileged sacrament. Through it the word becomes flesh and dwells among us.

CHAPTER 11

Mourning Our Barrenness

Several years ago, while teaching a summer course at Seattle University, I had as one of my students a woman who, while happily married, was unable to conceive a child. She had no illusions about what this meant for her. It bothered her a great deal. She found Mother's Day very difficult. Among other things, she wrote a well-researched thesis on the concept of barrenness in Scripture and developed a retreat on that same theme that she offered at various renewal centers.

Being a celibate whose vows also conscript a certain biological barrenness, I went on one of her weekend retreats, the only male there. It was a powerful group experience, but it took most of the weekend for that to happen. Initially most everyone on the retreat was tentative and shy, not wanting to admit to themselves or others the kind of pain the loss of biological parenthood was creating in their lives. But things broke open on the Saturday night, after the group watched a video of the 1990s British film *Secrets and Lies*, a subtle but powerful drama about the pain of not having children. The tears in the movie catalyzed tears within our group, and the floodgates opened. Tears began to flow freely, and one by one the women began to tell their stories. Then, after the tears and stories had stopped, the atmosphere changed, as if a fog had lifted and a weight had been removed. Lightness set in. Each person in the group had mourned her loss and now each felt a lightness in knowing that one might never have a child and still be a happy person, without denying the pain in that.

Barrenness is not just a term that describes a biological incapacity to have children or a life-choice to not have them. It's wider. Barrenness describes the universal human condition in its incapacity to be generative in the way it would like and the vacuum and frustration this leaves inside lives. No matter if we have biological children of our own or not, we still all find ourselves barren in that none of us are finished here on earth. There's always some barrenness left in our lives, and biological barrenness is simply one analogate of that, though arguably the prime one. None of us die having given birth to all we wanted to in this world.

What do we do in the face of this? Is there an answer? Is there a response that can take us beyond simply gritting our teeth and stoically getting on with it? There is. The answer is tears. In midlife and beyond, we need, as Alice Miller normatively suggests in a classic essay, "The Drama of the Gifted Child," to mourn so that our very foundations are shaken. Many of our wounds are irreversible and many of our shortcomings are permanent. We will go to our deaths with this incompleteness. Our loss cannot be reversed. But it can be mourned, both what we lost and what we failed to achieve. In that mourning there is freedom.

I have always been struck by the powerful metaphor inside the story of Jephthah's daughter in the biblical story in the Book of Judges that I described in chapter 4. It captures in an archetypal image the only answer there is, this side of eternity, to barrenness. Condemned to death in the prime of her youth by a foolish vow her father made, she tells her father that she is willing to die on the altar of sacrifice, but only on one condition. She will now die without experiencing either the consummation of marriage or the birthing of children. So, she asks her father to give her two months before her death to "mourn her virginity." Properly mourned, an incomplete life can be both lived in peace and left in peace.

Tears are the answer to barrenness, to all loss and inadequacy. Marilyn Chandler McEntyre, in her book *A Faithful Farewell*, has this to say about tears:

Tears release me into honest sorrow. They release
me from the strenuous business of finding words.
They release me into a childlike place where I need
to be held and find comfort in embrace—in the arms
of others and in the arms of God. Tears release me

from the treadmill of anxious thoughts, and even from fear. They release me from the strain of holding them back. Tears are a consent to what is. They wash away, at least for a time, denial and resistance. They allow me to relinquish the self-deceptive notion that I'm in control. Tears dilute resentment and wash away the flotsam left by waves of anger.[10]

Not insignificantly, tears are saltwater. Human life originated in the oceans. Tears connect us to the source of all life on this earth, within which prodigal fecundity trumps all barrenness.

CHAPTER 12

THE SACRAMENTALITY OF EVERYDAY LIFE

Christianity teaches us that our world is holy, that everything is matter for sacrament. In its view, the universe is a manifestation of God's glory, and humanity is made in God's image. Our bodies are temples of the Holy Spirit, the food we eat is sacramental, and in our work and in sexual embrace we are co-creators with God.

This is high theology, a symbolic hedge that dwarfs that found in virtually every other religion and philosophy. Nowhere else, save in outright pantheism, does anyone else affirm anything so radical that it borders on blasphemy. But this is Christian thought at its best.

The problem however is that, most times, our daily lives are so drab, distracted, and fixed upon realities that seem so base that it makes this idea ("everything is sacrament") seem adolescent fantasy. When we watch the news at night our world doesn't look like the glory of God; what we do with our bodies at times makes us wonder whether these really are temples of the Holy Spirit, the heartless and thankless way that we consume food and drink leaves little impression of sacramentality, and the symbols and language with which we surround our work and sex speak precious little of co-creation with God.

Why is this so? If the earth is ablaze with the fire of God, why do we, in the words of Elizabeth Barrett Browning, sit around and pick blackberries? What have we lost?

We have lost the sense that the world is holy and that our eating, working, and making love are sacramental; and we've lost it because we no longer have the right kind of prayer and ritual in our lives. We no longer connect ourselves, our world, and our eating and our making love, to their sacred origins. It is in not making this connection that our prayer and ritual fall short.

Let me try to illustrate this with a few examples:

Among the Osage Indians, there is a custom that when a child is born, before it is allowed to drink from its mother's breast, a holy person is summoned, someone "who has talked to the gods" is brought into the room. This person recites to the newborn infant the story of the creation of the world and of terrestrial animals. Not until this has been done is the baby given the mother's breast. Later, when the child is old enough to drink water, the same holy person is summoned again. This time he or she tells the story of creation, ending with the story of the sacred origins of water. Only then, after hearing this story, is the child given water. Then, when the child is old enough to take solid foods, "the person who talked to the gods" is brought in again and he or she, this time, tells the story of the origins of grains and other foods. The object of all of this is to introduce the newborn child into the sacramental reality of the world. This child will grow up to know that eating is not just a physiological act, but a religious one as well.

An older generation, that of my parents, had their own pious way of doing this ritual. They blessed their fields and workbenches and bedrooms, they prayed grace before and after every meal, and some of them went to finalize their engagement for marriage in a church. That was their way of telling the story of the sacred origins of water before drinking it.

By and large, we have rejected the mythological way of the Osage Indians and the pious way of my parents' generation. We live, eat, work, and make love under a lower symbolic hedge. Most of our eating isn't sacramental because we don't connect the food we eat to its sacred origins and, for the most part, we don't really pray before and after meals. Most of the time we consider our work as a job rather than as co-creation with God because we don't connect it to any sacred origins, and we don't bless our workbenches, offices, classrooms, and boardrooms. And our sex is rarely the Eucharist that it should be because the very thought of blessing a bedroom or having sacramental sex causes laughter in most contemporary circles.

I am not sure what the solution is. Our age isn't much for the mythology of ancient cultures or for the piety of more recent generations. The ways of the past, for better and for worse, are not our ways. But we must find a way . . . a way to connect our eating and our drinking, our working and our making love, to their sacred origins. Socrates once said that the unexamined life is not worth living. It is also not sacramental. Eating, working, and making love, without reflective prayer and proper ritual, are, in the end, drab and non-sacramental. The joylessness of so much that should bring us joy can tell us as much.

CHAPTER 13

UNDERSTANDING THE DESERT OF LONELINESS

Many summers ago, I decided to spend three months in a Trappist monastery. I was tired out from a very busy year within which my work kept me over-active, over-involved, and over-stimulated. I was looking for solitude, and in the weeks and days immediately preceding my departure for the monastery, I began more and more to fantasize about how good it was going to feel spending those months in solitude. I imagined myself walking in silence around a peaceful lake, sitting by a fireplace smoking a pipe, making visits to the chapel to pray, and sitting under an oak tree drinking in the serenity of the distant mountains.

I arrived at the monastery in the early afternoon and could hardly wait to begin all this solitude and . . . by late evening, I was restless and climbing the walls. I had already done almost all of the contemplative things about which I had fantasized. I had walked around the lake, smoked my pipe by the fireplace, visited the chapel twice, and sat under the oak tree and drunk in the mountains! Now I was in a panic, wondering what I would do for the rest of the summer—with no work to do, no meetings to go to, no classes to teach, no talks to give, no newspapers to read, no movies or television to watch, no picnics to go to with family and friends, no sports scores to watch over. I suddenly felt very sorry that I had gotten myself into this commitment. Also, at that moment—hyper, restless, dislocated, disillusioned, and in panic—I began to enter into solitude.

My case, I suspect, is typical. Our fantasy about solitude most often sees it precisely as leisured serenity, a quiet walk in the woods, a peaceful contemplation of some scene of beauty, or a consoling time spent sitting in a chapel or a church. The reality is, normally, exactly the opposite. Real solitude most often hits us unawares and sends us reeling. Almost always the initial stages of solitude are extremely painful and are experienced as dislocation, disillusionment, and intense loneliness. Moreover, like real prayer, genuine solitude is often not something we choose for ourselves. More often, solitude is the experience of being taken, against our own choosing, where we would rather not go.

We are led into solitude. Thus, for example, we are led into it in our experience of moral loneliness, namely, on those occasions when, alone or within a group, we feel ourselves radically isolated, a minority of one, in terms of what we hold precious and value deeply. It is when we feel most without moral companionship, when we feel out of sync with everyone else, dislocated, disillusioned, naked, and alone, that we are led into solitude. This is the desert that constitutes solitude, and it is always, initially, very painful—and it is rare that we go there of our own choosing. Most often we end up there after having exhausted every means of escaping the experience.

In John's Gospel (chapter 21), after Peter swears his love for him, Jesus tells Peter: "When you were younger, you used to dress yourself and go where you wanted; but when you grow old, you will stretch out your hands, and someone else will dress you and lead you where you do not want to go." John informs us that Jesus said this to indicate the type of death Peter was to die. Prayer and solitude are a lot about a certain kind of death—death to narcissism, to fantasy, to illusion, to false grandiosity, and to false beliefs and values. Rarely do we walk into the desert that purifies us of these by ourselves. Generally, it is a conspiracy of circumstances, more accurately called divine providence, that puts a rope around us and leads us where we would rather not go. Most of our solitude is by conscription. It is rarely by our active choosing that we are taken into the real desert.

This should, I hope, be valuable to us in helping us understand what is happening to us during those times when we feel so dislocated, isolated, alone, and morally lonely. We are experiencing desert pain, the rope of baptismal displacement that Jesus told Peter about, the dark night of the soul, the painful purification of real contemplation. Real solitude is not the type that one normally reads about in the tourist brochures . . . or that one fantasizes about when one is over-tired and over-restless! It is important, at those times when we are most lonely and in pain, to know this.

But it is this type of solitude that, because it is so disillusioning, precisely dispels illusion. It also dispels fantasy and narcissism because it takes us out of a dream world into the real world. And it is, ironically, this type of painful aloneness that is the basis for real community since, as Rainer Maria Rilke once said, love is the capacity of two solitudes to protect and border and greet each other.

CHAPTER 14

An Honest Anger

Today, for the main part, most of us live in chronic depression. This is not clinical depression, so it's not as if we need professional help or therapy, it's just that there is within our lives precious little in terms of delight.

We live and breathe within a culture and a church that are growing daily in sophistication, adultness, and criticalness. This is not always a bad thing, but it is helping to spawn a polarization, anger, and despondency that is making it almost unfashionable to be happy.

Much of this despondency has constellated around two centers: women's anger and men's grief.

As women touch gender issues, normally anger follows, much like smoke follows from fire. There is already within the popular mind the stereotype of the angry feminist. It's more than a stereotype. Many women who get in touch with gender issues do, in fact, get angry.

Interestingly, when men today touch their own gender issues, as they are doing today in men's circles, they have their own stereotypical reaction. They become sad and begin to grieve; so much so that today there is a new stereotype emerging within the popular mind that parallels the image of the angry feminist, namely, the grieving male.

Recently I addressed a national conference of Catholic journalists and tried to make the point that, as a Catholic press, we must address this despondency.

After my talk, I was challenged by a woman, a former teaching colleague and a longtime friend, who said to me: "Yes, I am angry, and so are many other women. But you make women's anger sound like something hard and calloused—while you make men's grief sound like something soft and sensitive. Is that really fair? Are they really that different? Isn't anger, in the end, just another form of grief?"

I was thankful for her challenge because, for the main part, she is right—anger and grief are not that different. On the surface, they appear antithetical, oil and vinegar, but examined more closely, most of the time they are expressions of the same thing: love that's been wounded and yearns for reconciliation.

Rollo May famously suggested that the opposite of love is not hate or anger. The opposite of love is indifference. You can only really hate or be properly and thoroughly angry with somebody that you love.

The deeper the love, the deeper will be the anger and hatred if the love is wounded or betrayed. Anger and hatred, initially at least, are almost always a sure sign of love. They are love's grief. Most anger, in the end, is a form of grief . . . just

58 THE FIRE WITHIN

as most grief, when boiled down to its essentials, is a form of anger.

But not all anger is good, and neither are all forms of grief. There are different kinds of anger, and these have parallel kinds of grief. There is honest anger and there is dishonest anger, there is honest grief and there is dishonest grief.

Let me try to explain this, using anger. Grief has identical parallels. Honest anger obeys three rules:

* First, it does not distort. Good anger does not let hurt blind one to what was good in the past so as to allow a revisionist distortion of the truth. Honest anger is real anger; it feels and points out what is wrong, but it doesn't, on that account, lie about what is and what was good. It lets the good remain good.
* Second, it is not rage. There is a big difference between honest anger and rage. Despite its rather coarse surface and its painful disturbing of the peace, honest anger, in the end, seeks to build up, to bring to a new wholeness, to reconcile something that is felt as fractured or broken. It is a disruptive means toward a good end.

  Rage, by contrast, wants only to bring down, to break apart, to utterly destroy. Its wound is so deep that there is no more desire for unity and reconciliation. The clearest expression of this is murder/suicide, the case where the wounded lover kills his lost love and then kills himself.

* Finally, honest anger has a time limit; it is not forever. It howls and wails for "40 days," the length of time needed, and then it moves on to the promised land. Honest anger never sees itself as an end, a substitute for the lost love.

It does not make an ideology of itself ("I am unhappy . . . and I have every right to be!"). Like the Israelites in the desert, like a pining lover, its every energy seeks for the road beyond, the way out, reconciliation, an embrace that heals the fracture.

Honest grief follows the same rules—and these are important rules for all of us, women and men, who desire to move beyond the present divisions to a new embrace.

CHAPTER 15

DESIRE INTO PRAYER

For some years now, an Oblate colleague of mine has been developing an idea he calls "The Evangelization of Desire." Among other things, he gives a retreat to help people get in touch with their deep desires so as to see in them how the Holy Spirit prays through their longing.

In essence, he tries to help people appropriate in a personal way what St. Paul says when he tells us that when we do not know how to pray as we should, the Spirit, "with groaning too deep for words," prays through us.

How does the Spirit pray through human longing? There is a complex, though very rich, theological explanation for this. At its root lies the fact that the same Holy Spirit who drove Jesus into the desert and guided him through his ministry also drives all of physical creation, including the movements of the heart. What animated Jesus also animates everything else, except that nothing else is as perfectly responsive to it as Jesus was.

The Holy Spirit is the deep fire driving all of creation, and the dynamics of this spirit can be studied through physics, biology, chemistry, or psychology, just as they can be studied through Christology and spirituality. As the Psalmist puts it in Psalm 104, addressing God, "if you take away your spirit, all creation returns to dust." Astonishing? Yes.

The Holy Spirit holds physical creation together. What animates the union of hydrogen and oxygen and what animated Jesus is the same thing, a spirit that unites elements and then presses outward towards greater life, a fire that can be seen in Jesus's life and ministry, just as it can be seen in the relentless growth of a bamboo plant. At the heart of everything there is a divine fire. In the end, all yearning, longing, and aching, every desire we have, is driven by that fire. So too are the laws of gravity.

And what does this fire want? An interesting question. Jesus poses it to us at the beginning of John's Gospel and then answers at the end of that Gospel.

In the first chapter of John, Jesus sees two persons eyeing him with curiosity and he asks them: "What are you looking for?" At the end of the Gospel, he answers the question. When Mary Magdala comes looking for his dead body and meets instead his resurrected person, he pronounces her name: "Mary." In that, she recognizes him, and she recognizes too what she, and everyone else and all of creation, is wanting, namely, to have God, personally and gently, pronounce her name. What are we looking for? All of the fire in all of creation, all conscious and unconscious desire, in the end, longs to be so embraced by God, to have God intimately pronounce its name.

But—and this needs to be immediately added—this has already happened; God has already pronounced our names. In the depths of the soul, in that part of us where all that is most precious is kept and nurtured, where we suffer moral loneliness, where we have our purest longings, we know that we have already been touched, caressed, and embraced by God. There is a part of us that no hurt can harden, no abuse can stain, and no sin (save the sin against the Holy Spirit) can warp. It is here that we have a dark, warm memory of having once been gently embraced, held, and caressed.

An ancient legend says that, before putting a soul into a person, God kisses that soul. Bernard Lonergan suggests that faith is "the brand of God" inside of us, an indelible memory of some deep touch. These are other ways of speaking of this.

There is a place in the soul where we still remember feeling God's embrace, and it is there that we gently hear God call our name whenever in this life we meet truth, love, gentleness, forgiveness, justice, and innocence. In the presence of these the soul feels right, something touches its hypothalamus, and we, like Mary of Magdala, suddenly recognize the voice of Christ calling our name.

So how do we evangelize desire? How can we take the aching dis-ease within us and turn it into prayer? How do we baptize what groans in us and what groans in creation?

By nurturing more and more that part in us that still remembers God's embrace, by getting in touch with our moral loneliness, by recognizing that all that is so restless in us wants, at its root, to hear God call its name, and by connecting truth, love, gentleness, forgiveness, justice, and innocence with the voice of the resurrected Christ.

CHAPTER 16

WAITING

In her novel *The Underpainter*, Jane Urquhard offers some thoughts on waiting. Her main character, a brilliant artist whose capacity to live and relate healthily does not parallel his aesthetic talents, tells of a conversation he has had with Sara, his woman-friend of sixteen years:

> Sometime during August of 1935, the last month of the last summer I spent at Sliver Islet, Sara told me what it was like to wait. She said that there were two kinds of waiting: the waiting that consumes the mind and that which occurs somewhere below the surface of awareness. The latter is more bearable, but also more dangerous because it manifests itself in ways that are not at first definable as such. She told me that over the period of the last winter she had finally realized that everything that she did or said— every activity—was either a variant of, or a substitute for, waiting and therefore had no relevance on its own.[11]

An interesting reflection. Henri Nouwen used to say that 98 percent of our lives are spent in waiting. At a superficial level, we experience this in the amount of time we spend waiting at check-out counters, in airports, for buses, for somebody to arrive, or for something to end—our workday, a class, a church service, a meal, a family discussion, a bout with the flu. But that is the superficial part of it.

More important is the fact that almost all the time we are waiting for a fuller season for our lives. Rarely do we have what Nouwen calls "a fully pregnant moment," namely, a moment when we can say to ourselves: "Right now, I don't want to be any other place, with any other persons, doing anything else, than what I am doing right now!"

From infancy onwards, we are nearly always waiting for something else to happen: When we are babies, every time our mother leaves the room we wait anxiously for her to return. As a child, we wait for those special moments of play and celebration—"When will Gramma come? When will my friend visit again? When will it be time to eat? When will I get my treat? When will it be Christmas? When will we get to go to the park again?" Little children are not satisfied for long.

This changes somewhat during pre-adolescence. The years between starting school and puberty are perhaps the one time in life when we are more satisfied with the present moment. In those years before our sexual awakening, we see things less through the prism of dis-ease. However, even in this period, there is a constant restlessness, for we want to grow up, be like the big kids, be independent, do grown-up things.

Then at puberty, the awakening of sexuality arouses within us a restlessness that makes the rest of our lives one painful exercise in waiting. From that moment onwards, every hormone in us longs for a consummation that, even if it is ever attained, is had only for the briefest of moments. Moreover, sexuality also stirs the soul, rousing within us a longing ("below the surface of awareness") that makes virtually every activity for the rest of our lives precisely "either a variant of, or a substitute for, waiting" and an activity that does not have full relevance on its own.

For a while, of course, this is a waiting that consumes the mind: We want to meet the right person, fall in love, get married, have children, achieve something significant, create something lasting, gain the respect of family and peers, create some independence, and acquire the good things of life. But Urquhart is right. Something else, something under the surface of awareness, is driving all of this, and the things we so long for on the surface, good in themselves, do not have full relevance on their own.

But if this is true, isn't there something fundamentally wrong here? Isn't the task of life precisely that of making the present moment enough? Doesn't the wisdom of the ages tell us to seize the day? Isn't it rather stoic and joy-killing to accept that life is 98 percent about waiting?

On the contrary, to accept that in this life all symphonies remain unfinished is not masochistic, but freeing. My parents' generation did this by, each day, saying the prayer: "For now we live, mourning and weeping in this valley of tears." Praying like this didn't turn them into cold stoics. Instead, knowing that the full symphony for which we wait cannot be had here, they were able to enjoy, perhaps more so than can our own generation, the real joys that are possible.

Carl Jung once said that life is a journey between the paradise of the womb and the paradise of heaven. Jesus said that while on earth we are on pilgrimage. Is it any wonder then that at a certain point in life we begin to realize that everything is a variant of, or a substitute for, waiting?

CHAPTER 17

RE-IMAGINING CHASTITY

In her marvelous little book *Holy the Firm*, Annie Dillard describes how she once learned a fundamental lesson about life simply by watching a moth emerge from its cocoon. She had been fascinated watching the nearly imperceptible process of metamorphosis but, at a point, it became too slow for her. To speed up things a little, she applied a tiny bit of heat from a candle to the cocoon. It worked. The extra heat quickened the process and the moth emerged a bit sooner than it would have otherwise. However, because nature had not been able to take its full course, the moth was born damaged, its wings unable to form fully.[12]

What Dillard describes here is a violation of chastity. Properly understood, chastity is precisely a question of having the patience to bear the tension of the interminable slowness of things. To be chaste is to not prematurely force things so that everybody and everything, each within its own unique rhythm, is properly respected.

That is normally not the way we think of chastity. Generally, we relate chastity to sex, more particularly, to the lack of it. For most of us, chastity means celibacy—and celibacy, in our culture, suggests an unenviable innocence, an ignorance, really, a missing out on the most central thing in life. Chastity, as we know, is not very popular in our culture, partly because we conceive of it so badly. What is it?

Chastity is not first and foremost a sexual concept. It has to do with the way we relate to reality in general. In essence, chastity is proper reverence and respect. To be chaste is to stand before reality, everything and everybody, and fully respect the proper contours and rhythm of things.

To be chaste then means to let things unfold as they should. Thus it means, among many other things, to not open our gifts before Christmas, to not rush our own or our children's growth, to not experience things for which we aren't ready, to not lose patience in life or in sex because there is tension, to not violate someone else's beauty and sexuality, to not apply a candle to a moth emerging from its cocoon because we're in a hurry, and to not sleep with the bride before the wedding. To be chaste is to let gift be gift. Biblically, to be chaste is to have our shoes off before the burning bush.

Chastity is reverence and respect. All irreverence and disrespect is the antithesis of chastity.

Chastity as a practical virtue is then predicated on two things: patience and the capacity to carry tension.

Patience is basically synonymous with chastity. To fully respect others and the proper order of things means to be patient. Something can be wrong for no other reason than that it is premature. To do anything too quickly, whether that be growing up, or having sex, does what applying extra heat does to the process of metamorphosis. It leaves us with damaged wings.

Allan Bloom, the renowned late philosopher of education, in describing lack of chastity in today's youth, put things this way: Premature experience is bad precisely because it is premature. In youth, for example, yearning is meant precisely for sublimation, in the sense of making things sublime, of orientating what aches in us toward great love, great art, and great achievement. Premature experience, like the false ecstasy of drugs, artificially induces the exaltation naturally attached to the completion of some great endeavor—victory in a just war, mature consummated love, great artistic creation, real religious devotion, and the discovery of deep truth. Premature experience has precisely the effect of clipping our wings in that it drains us of great enthusiasm and great expectations. Great longing then becomes little more than being horny. Only sublimation, tension, and waiting (the proper definition of patience) allow for the sublime.

The capacity to carry tension is too an integral part of chastity. To properly respect others, to have the patience to not act prematurely, requires that we be willing and able to carry tension and to carry it for a long time, perhaps even for a lifetime. To wait in tension, in incompleteness, in longing, in frustration, in inconsummation, and in helplessness in the face of the interminable slowness of things, especially in the face of how slow love and justice seem to appear in our lives, is to practice chastity.

When Jesus sweated blood in the Garden of Gethsemane, he was practicing chastity; just as when Mary stood under the cross, unable to stop its senselessness and unable even to protest Jesus's innocence, she too was practicing chastity. Unless we are willing to carry tension, in the same way, we will, precisely, never wait for the wedding night.

Chastity's challenge reads this way: Never short-circuit the process of metamorphosis. Whether you are dealing with sex or with life in general, wait for the wedding night for the consummation.

CHAPTER 18

WHAT IS PURITY?

In the early 1950s, Michel Quoist wrote a book in French that was translated into English a decade later, titled *Prayers of Life*. It became immensely popular. The book combined rare depth with a language bordering on poetry. It remains one of the true spiritual classics of the last century. One of its prayers speaks of our struggle for purity—purity of heart, of body, of intention, and includes these lines:

> I've given you all, but it's hard, Lord.
> It's hard to give one's body, it would like to give itself
>   to others.
> It's hard to love everyone and claim no one.
> It's hard to shake a hand and not want to retain it.
> It's hard to inspire affection, only to give it to you.
> It's hard to be nothing to oneself in order to be everything
>   to others.
> It's hard to be like others, among others, but to be other.
> It's hard always to give without trying to receive.
> It's hard to seek out others and be, oneself, unsought. . . . [13]

That describes perhaps our deepest struggle in life and in love. We struggle with purity, though we rarely admit it.

Today the word *purity* has taken on mainly negative connotations. It's understood as a sexual concept and is mostly seen as negative. For many people it connotes fear, timidity, and a certain uptightness about sex and life. The popular culture almost ridicules purity, and it's rare that a critically acclaimed movie, a major novel, or a renowned artist captures its essence aesthetically, celebrates its beauty, and challenges us with its importance.

That's sad, really, because our lack of purity is, I believe, one of the deep causes of sadness in our lives. There's a difference, as we know, between pleasure and happiness. Bracketing purity can sometimes be the route to pleasure, but it's never a road to happiness. Lack of purity always brings sadness.

What is purity? First of all, it's not primarily about sex, though because our sexual desires are so powerful we often compromise our purity in sex. And here, despite all our claims of how free and liberated we are, we still sense the value of purity, however inchoately. Indeed, the idea that sex is somehow dirty never quite disappears. Deep down, we still long for purity, though mostly we don't understand what we're longing for. What we long for is not immunity from the earthiness of sex, but purity of heart, chastity of intention. The deep-seated idea that sex is dirty has, I suspect, more to do with millennia of bad hygiene than with the aesthetics and morality of sex. Sex isn't bad, but our intentions can be.

"Blessed are the pure of heart, they shall see God!" Those words come from Jesus and contain more challenge than we imagine. Purity isn't just a route we need to travel if we want to see God, it's also a practical secret for tasting happiness in this life. Purity is what takes manipulation out of our relationships and sadness out of our lives. How?

Purity is not so much about sex as it is about intention. We need a certain purity and chastity of intention or we will always manipulate others in everything, including sex. We are pure when our hearts don't greedily or prematurely grab what isn't theirs. As Quoist so aptly puts it, we are pure when we can grasp a hand and not try to retain it, when we can love without being over-possessive, serve without being manipulative, and when we no longer try to make other people orbit around us as their center. We are pure when we stop using others for our own enhancement, whatever that might be. We become more pure as we become less manipulative in relationships.

But that's hard to do. It's hard to do in love and sex because of the fierce, restless, and sometimes obsessive desires and jealousies we feel there. But it's hard to be pure in any aspect of our lives. We live with such powerful desires to drink in everything and everybody that it's easy to be manipulative, to be blind to what we're doing to others as we struggle to create meaning, pleasure, and power for ourselves. It's easy to have a sense of entitlement, to be angry, to be bitter, to be jealous, to be driven by the search for pleasure or power, to use others for our own enhancement, to be so addicted to the pursuit of experience and sophistication that we sacrifice even our happiness on that altar. It's easy to be impure.

And it's also easy to be sad and unhappy, right within the experience of pleasure. Impurity can bring a certain richness of experience, a certain sophistication, and a certain pleasure. Adam and Eve's eyes were opened, not closed, after their sin, and one suspects, despite the pictures in our early catechisms, that their new-found sophistication helped block any real remorse. Impurity does open one's eyes. But it also brings a certain sadness, a cynicism, a split inside of ourselves, and a lack of self-worth into our lives.

Having a sense of our own dignity is predicated upon a certain purity. Impurity never lets us feel good about ourselves.

CHAPTER 19

LIVING WITH FEELING AND SOUL

"Repent and believe in the good news!" These are the first words out of Jesus's mouth in Mark's Gospel, and they are meant as a summary of the entire gospel. But what do these words mean?

In English, the word "repent" is often misunderstood. It seems to imply that we have already done something wrong, regret it, and now commit ourselves to live in a new way. Repentance, understood in this way, means to live beyond a sinful past. Biblically, this is not quite what is meant. In the Gospels, the particular word used for repentance is *metanoia*. Literally this means to do an about face, to turn around, to face in an entirely new direction. But what direction?

Bishop Robert Barron, when he was a young theologian in Mundelein, offered a simple, yet profound, understanding of this. He taught that within each of us there are two souls, a little soul (a *pusilla anima*) and a great soul (a *magna anima*). On any given day we tend to identify more with one or the other of these, and we are a very different person depending upon which soul is reigning within us.

Thus, if I take my identity from my little soul, I will inevitably feel bitter and angry. It is here, in the *pusilla anima*, where I am petty, afraid, aware of my hurts, and constantly nursing the sense of having been cheated and short-changed. In my little soul, I am paranoid and defensive. When I relate to life through it, I am short-sighted, impatient, despairing, and constantly looking for compensation.

But I also have within me a great soul. When I let it reign, I become a different person altogether. I am relating out of my great soul at those moments when I am overwhelmed by compassion, when everyone is brother or sister to me, when I want to give of myself without concern of cost, when I am able to carry the tensions of life without a breakdown in my chastity, when I would willingly die for others, and when my arms and my heart would want nothing other than to embrace the whole world and everyone in it.

All of us, I am sure, have had ample experience of both, identifying with the great soul and with the petty soul within us. Sometimes we operate out of one, sometimes out of the other.

When Jesus asks us to "repent," to do *metanoia*, what he is asking is that we cease identifying ourselves with the little soul and instead begin to live out of our other soul, the *magna anima*. The very etymology of the word *metanoia* implies this. It takes its root in two Greek words: *meta*—beyond; and *nous*—mind. Literally, *metanoia* means to move beyond our present mindset, beyond our present way of seeing things.

When one looks at the miracles of Jesus, it is interesting to see that so many of them are connected to opening up or otherwise healing someone's eyes, ears, or tongue. These miracles, of course, always have more than a physical significance. Eyes are opened in order to see more deeply and spiritually; ears are opened in order to hear things more compassionately; and tongues are loosened in order to praise God more freely and to speak words of reconciliation and love to each other. To put it metaphorically, what Jesus is doing in these miracles is attaching the eyes, ears, and tongue to the great soul so that what a person is now seeing, hearing, and speaking is not bitterness, hurt, and pettiness but rather compassion, gratitude, and praise.

Many of us are familiar with a famous passage in Thomas Merton within which he describes a revelation he had one day while standing on the corner of Fourth and Walnut in Louisville. Among complete strangers in the middle of a shopping district on a very ordinary day, Merton had the sense that his eyes, ears, and tongue were suddenly attached to a bigger soul:

I was suddenly overwhelmed with the realization that I loved all of those people, that they were mine, and I, theirs, that we could not be alien to one another even though we were total strangers. It was like waking from a dream of separateness. . . . Then it was as if I suddenly saw the secret beauty of their hearts, the depths of their hearts, where neither sin, nor desire, nor self-knowledge, can reach the core of their reality, the person that each one is in God's eyes. If only we could all see each other that way all the time! There would be no more war, no more hatred, no more cruelty, no more greed. I suppose that the big problem would be that we would all fall down and worship each other.[14]

To repent is let the great soul, the image and likeness of God, reign within us so that, like Merton on the corner of Fourth and Walnut, we are so overwhelmed with compassion that indeed we do turn and face in a completely new direction.

CHAPTER 20

A Plea for the Soul

It's hard to find your soulmate in someone who doesn't believe you have a soul.

Recently on *The Moth Radio Hour* a young woman shared the story of her breakup with her boyfriend, a young man for whom she had deep feelings. The problem was that she, a person with a deep faith, a Mormon, struggled with the radical materialism of her boyfriend. For him, there were no souls; the physical world was real, and nothing else. She kept asking him if he believed he had a soul. He couldn't make himself believe that. Eventually, not without a lot of heartache, they broke up. Why? In her words: "It's hard to find your soulmate in someone who doesn't believe you have a soul."

Her frustration is becoming more universal. More and more our world is ignoring and denying the existence of soul, becoming soulless. It wasn't always like this. Up until modern times, often it was the physical and the body that weren't properly honored. But things have changed, radically.

It began with Darwin, who rooted our origins more in the history of our bodies than in the origins of our souls; it took more shape in the mechanistic philosophies of the last century, which understood both our universe and ourselves as physical machines; it became more firm as modern medicine and experimental psychology began more and more to explain the brain primarily in terms of carbon complexification and biochemical interactions; it seeped into our higher educational systems as we produced more and more technical schools rather than universities in the deeper sense; and it culminated in popular culture where love and sex are spoken of more in terms of chemistry than in terms of soul. It is not surprising that for most pop singers today the mantra is: I want your body! I want your body! We're a long way from Shakespeare's marriage of true minds and Yeats's love of the pilgrim soul in you.

Religion of course has always lodged its protests against this, but often its understanding of the soul was itself too narrow to have much power to lure a materialistic culture back into wanting to rediscover and listen to the soul. Ironically, it took a nonreligious figure, Carl Jung, to speak of soul again in a way that is intellectually intriguing. And it was in the sick, the insane, the suicidal, and others whose lives were broken that Jung began to hear the cry of the soul (whose demands are sometimes very different from those of the body and whose needs are for much more than simple comfort and the prolonging of life).

Much of Jung's teaching and that of his followers can be seen as a protest for the soul. We see this, for example, in the writing of James Hillman. It's ironic that as an agnostic he was able to speak about the soul in ways that we who are religious might envy and emulate. Like Jung, he also drew many of his insights from listening to the soul cry out its meaning and pain through the voices of the sick, the insane, the broken, and the suicidal. Religion, medicine, and psychology, he believes, are not hearing the soul's cry. They're forever trying to fix the soul, cure the soul, or save the soul, rather than listening to the soul, which wants and needs neither to be fixed nor saved. It's already eternal. The soul needs to be heard and heard in all its godly goodness and earthy complexes. And sometimes what it tells us goes against all common sense, medical practice, and the oversimplistic spiritualities we often present as religion.

To be more in touch with our souls we might examine an older language, the language that religion, poets, mythologists, and lovers used before today's dominant materialism turned our language about the soul into the language of chemistry and mechanism. We cannot understand the soul through any scientific description but only by looking at its behavior, its insatiability, its dissatisfactions, and its protests. A soul isn't explained, it's experienced, and soul experience always comes soaked in depth, in longing, in eros, in limit, in the feeling of being pilgrim in need of a soulmate.

Happily, even today, we still do spontaneously connect the soul to things beyond chemistry and mechanism. As

Hillman points out: "We associate the word 'soul' with: mind, spirit, heart, life, warmth, humanness, personality, individuality, intentionality, essence, innermost, purpose, emotion, quality, virtue, morality, sin, wisdom, death, God. As well, we speak of a soul as 'troubled,' 'old,' 'disembodied,' 'immortal,' 'lost,' 'innocent,' 'inspired.' Eyes are said to be 'soulful,' for the eyes are 'the mirror of the soul'; and one can be 'soulless' by showing no mercy."[15]

Soullessness: We understand the make-up of something best when we see it broken. So perhaps today we can best understand our soullessness in the growing acceptance of pornography and hook-up sex, where the soul is intentionally and necessarily excluded from what is meant to be the epitome of all soulful experience.

CHAPTER 21

A Lonely Place from Which to Pray and Speak

Robert Coles once wrote a fine biographical essay on Simone Weil. In it, he coined a beautiful phrase to describe a quality that made her so extraordinary and that also caused her much suffering in her adult life. "Moral loneliness," he called it.[16]

Poets, novelists, mystics, and philosophers have always, in their different ways, spoken of this: Thus, for example, the German poet Goethe speaks of "the desire for higher lovemaking"; the Czech novelist Ivan Klima talks about "knowing how to bear your solitude at a great height"; another Czech writer, Milan Kundera, speaks of "resisting the great march"; and Jesus, the Gospels tell us, used to go off "to the lonely place" to be by himself. Each of these expressions is speaking about a certain feeling, but it is also speaking about a certain place in the soul, namely, that part where you are most yourself, most true to yourself, most alone, and most lonely—that part of your soul where would you most need someone to sleep with but where generally you sleep alone. What is meant by all this?

More than twenty years ago, now, Olivier Todd wrote a biography on Albert Camus, the French existentialist who won the Nobel Prize for literature. The portrait Todd gives us of Camus in *Albert Camus: A Life* is not a particularly pious one; hardly the stuff of hagiography. Camus, it turns out, had his weaknesses, including his share of irresponsibility in personal relations. Yet, despite that, what emerges in the end is the picture of a noble man, a great soul, an extraordinary moral creature. Why? Precisely because, whatever his other faults, Camus, like Simone Weil, always bore his solitude at a great height; like Jesus (albeit in a different way) he often went off by himself to the lonely place. In Camus's life there was always a structural innocence even when he wasn't always innocent in his private life. Why do I say this?

Because throughout his whole life, he always stood apart from the crowd—not in the sense that he asserted his individuality so as to make a statement with his life— but in the moral sense. He was always the one defending the outsider against the crowd, a minority-of-one resisting the surge of the mob. Thus, when the Nazis overran France and many of his colleagues, because of fear or personal advantage, collaborated, he held out, at great danger to himself. Later, after the war, when Marxism became fashionable among his intellectual friends (including Sartre), he resisted it, pointing out its inconsistencies, violence, and narrowness, even though this cost him a lot of popularity and some key friends. This was his pattern in everything; he took the road less traveled. Against suffocating clerics, he asserted the freedom of the human mind; then, against narrow atheism, he turned around and asserted the central importance of the question of God's existence. Always he stood against the mob, against the great hammer of popular acclaim, ever suspicious of the pervasive ideology, of the political correctness of both the right and the left. Because of this, most of the time he stood alone, without friends, unanimity-minus-one. There is an irony here. Camus was hardly a celibate, but, where it counted most, he slept alone. He was morally single.

It's people like him, and Simone Weil, that we most need in the world and the church today. There is a want for persons, especially leaders, who can bear their solitude at such a height, who can stand solitary against the prevailing ideologies and political correctness of both the right and the left, and speak and minister out of that lonely place; persons who can be unanimity-minus-one. We don't have enough individuals like Simone Weil and Albert Camus around today. We have enough pretense of high solitude— more than enough unhappy persons who confuse truth with personal anger, ideologies of the right and the left, political correctness, or the surge of a mob. It's easy enough to be part of a great march, but, like Weil and Camus, can we be just as critical of our own? Can we challenge our fellow marchers with the truth in the position of those we are marching against? Not easily done; mostly because it's a quick way to lose friends and popularity, not to mention your membership card in whatever movement within which you happen to be marching.

To bear one's solitude at a high level is to exalt the freedom of the human spirit, even as you genuflect in obedience to a sovereign God; to celebrate the fire of passion, even as you defend the beauty of chastity; to defend what is best in liberal ideology about women, ecology, and racism, even as you defend what is best in conservative belief regarding the importance of family, sexual boundaries, and private morality. To bear your solitude at a high level is, however, to find yourself morally lonely, sleeping alone in that area where you would most need intimacy, and praying from that desert that Jesus frequented, "the lonely place."

CHAPTER 22

What We Long For

Recently after a lecture, I was confronted by an angry man who accused me of being soft on God's judgment and justice. Though angry, he was a good man, someone who had given his life in duty to family, church, country, and God.

"I cannot accept what you say," he muttered bitterly. "There's so much evil in the world and so many people are suffering from other peoples' sins that there must be retribution, some justice. Don't tell me that the people who are doing these things—from molesting children to ignoring all morality—are going to be in heaven when we get there! What would that say about God's justice?"

I don't deny the existence of hell, nor of the importance of God's judgment, but the itch to see other people suffer retribution reveals, I believe, things about ourselves that we might not want to admit.

But at least we're in good company: The prophet Isaiah was no different. For him it was not enough that the Messiah should usher in heaven for good people. Along with rewards for the good, he felt, there needed to be too a "day of vengeance" on the bad (Isaiah 61:2). Interestingly, in a curious omission, when Jesus quotes this text to define his own ministry, he leaves out the part about vengeance (Luke 4:18).

Too many of us today, conservatives and liberals alike, have a need to see punishment befall the wicked. It is not enough that eventually the good should have its day and that we should be rewarded. No, the bad must also be punished. Liberals and conservatives might disagree on what constitutes sin and wickedness, but they tend to agree that it must be punished.

To my mind, this desire for justice (as we call it) is not always healthy, and, in a way, it speaks volumes about a certain frustration and bitterness within our own lives. All that worry that somebody might be getting away with something and all that anxiety that God might not be an exacting judge, suggest that we, like the older brother of the prodigal son, might be doing a lot of things right, but are missing something important inside of ourselves. We are dutiful and moral, but bitter underneath and thus unable to enter the circle of celebration and the dance. Everything about us is right, except for the lack of real warmth in our hearts.

Julian of Norwich once described God this way: "Completely relaxed and courteous, he himself was the happiness and peace of his dear friends, his beautiful face radiating measureless love like a marvelous symphony."

That is one of the better descriptions of God written, but it can make for a painful meditation: Too often, for too many of us, far from basking in gratitude in the beauty of relaxed, measureless love, and infinite forgiveness that make up heaven, we feel instead the bitterness, self-pity, anger, and incapacity to let go and dance that was felt by the older brother of the prodigal son. We are inside the banquet room, amongst all the radiance and joy, but we are unhappy, pouting, waiting for the Father to come and try to coax us beyond our sense of having been cheated. Such is too often the feeling among us, good people: Like the older brother of the prodigal son, we protest our right to despair, to be unhappy, and we demand that a reckoning justice one day give us our due by punishing the bad.

The famous Swiss psychologist Alice Miller suggests that the primary spiritual task of the second half of life is dealing with this. We need to grieve, she says, or the bitterness and anger that come from our wounds, disappointments, bad choices, and broken dreams will overwhelm us with a sense of life's unfairness. Her formula for health is simple: Life is unfair. Don't try to protect yourself from its hurts—You've already been hurt! Accept that, grieve it, and move on to rejoin the dance.

In the end, it's mostly because we are wounded and bitter that we worry about God's justice, that it might be too lenient, that the bad will not be fully punished. But we should worry less about that and more about our own incapacity to forgive, to let go of our hurts, to take delight in life, to give others the gaze of admiration, to celebrate, and to join in the dance. To be fit for heaven we must let go of bitterness.

Like the older brother, our problem is ultimately not the undeserved and excessive love that is seemingly shown to someone else. Our problem is more that we have never really heard in our hearts the gentle words that the Father spoke to the older brother: "My child, you have always been with me and all I have is yours, but we, you and I, need to be happy and dance because your younger brother was dead and has come back to life!"

ACKNOWLEDGMENTS

Nobody gives birth alone. There is generally a midwife there. So some thanks are in order.

First, I would like to thank Jon Sweeney at Paraclete Press for his initiative, his prodding, his advice, and his patience in working with me in bringing this book to birth. Thanks too to Robert Edmonson at Paraclete Press for his editing and his patience.

Most of the substance of this book is extracted from various newspaper columns that I have written in recent years. There are too many people to thank here, but I would like to single out one for special thanks, namely, Glen Argan (*Western Catholic Reporter*) who, thirty-eight years ago, was the first editor to take a chance on me. Thank you, Glen, for being the first midwife.

Beyond this, I want to thank my various families: the community here at *Oblate School of Theology* who have given me a nurturing home for more than fifteen years; my blood family, that large amorphous tribe that continues to love me despite geographical distance and my absences; my Oblate family, the *Missionary Oblates of Mary Immaculate*, for their trust in me; and the family of friends who support me more than I deserve. As they say here in Texas: *Thank you all!*

Finally, and not least, I want to thank you, the reader, for picking up this book. Every writer, if he or she is humble, knows that when one writes, all one is doing is putting notes into bottles and floating them out to sea with the hope that someone finds them and reads them. Thank you for picking up this bottle and this particular note!

ABOUT THE AUTHOR

Ronald Rolheiser, OMI, is a specialist in the fields of spirituality and systematic theology. His regular column in the *Catholic Herald* is featured in newspapers in five different countries. He is the author of many books, including bestsellers such as *The Holy Longing*, as well as *The Restless Heart*, *Forgotten Among the Lilies*, and *Bruised and Wounded: Struggling to Understand Suicide* and *Domestic Monastery* with Paraclete Press. He lives in San Antonio, Texas, where he is president of the Oblate School of Theology.

NOTES

1 Karl Rahner, article on *Man, Anthropology, Theological,* in *Sacramentum Mundi,* Volume Three (New York: Herder and Herder, 1969), 365–70.

2 Karl Rahner, *Servants of the* Lord (New York: Herder and Herder, 1968), 152.

3 T. S. Eliot, from "Little Gidding," IV, lines 13-14, the last of the *Four Quartets,* www.davidgorman.com/4quartets/4-gidding.htm.

4 See particularly Ronald Rolheiser, *Forgotten Among the Lilies: Learning to Love Beyond Our Fears* (New York: Image, 2007).

5 See Michael Meade's essays at mosaicvoices.org.

6 Gordon Lightfoot, from the album *Don Quixote,* Reprise Records – MS 2056, ℗© 1972-Warner Bros. Records Inc.

7 See my book, *Sacred Fire: A Vision for a Deeper Human and Christian Maturity* (New York: Image, 2017).

8 Ruth Burrows, *Before the Living God* (Denville, NJ: Dimension, 1975), 5.

9 C. S. Lewis, *The Problem of Pain* (New York: HarperOne, 2015), 14.

10 Marilyn Chandler McEntyre, *A Faithful Farwell: Living Your Last Chapter with Love* (Grand Rapids, MI: Eerdmans, 2015), 78.

11 Jane Urquhart, *The Underpainter* (New York: Penguin, 1998), 95.

12 Annie Dillard, *Holy the Firm* (New York: Harper Perennial, 1998), 13–18.

13 "The Priest: A Prayer on Sunday Night," from Michel Quoist, *Prayers of Life,* trans. Anne Marie de Commaille and Agnes Mitchell Forsyth (Toronto: Gill and Macmillan, 1963), 64–68. More recently, see Michel Quoist, *Prayers, revised edition* (Kansas City, MO: Sheed and Ward, 1985).

14 Thomas Merton, *Conjectures of a Guilty Bystander* (New York: Image Books, 2009), 153.

15 James Hillman, *The Essential James Hillman: A Blue Fire,* introduced and edited by Thomas Moore (East Sussex, UK: Routledge, 1998), 19–20.

16 Robert Coles, *Simone Weil: A Modern Pilgimage* (Woodstock, VT: SkyLight Paths Publishing, 2001), chapter 5.

ABOUT PARACLETE PRESS

As the publishing arm of the Community of Jesus, Paraclete Press presents a full expression of Christian belief and practice—from Catholic to Evangelical, from Protestant to Orthodox, reflecting the ecumenical charism of the Community and its dedication to sacred music, the fine arts, and the written word. We publish books, recordings, sheet music, and video/DVDs that nourish the vibrant life of the church and its people.

WHAT WE ARE DOING

BOOKS | PARACLETE PRESS BOOKS show the richness and depth of what it means to be Christian. While Benedictine spirituality is at the heart of who we are and all that we do, our books reflect the Christian experience across many cultures, time periods, and houses of worship.

We have many series, including *Paraclete Essentials*; *Paraclete Fiction*; *Paraclete Poetry*; *Paraclete Giants*; and for children and adults, *All God's Creatures*, books about animals and faith; and *San Damiano Books*, focusing on Franciscan spirituality. Others include *Voices from the Monastery* (men and women monastics writing about living a spiritual life today), *Active Prayer*, and new for young readers: *The Pope's Cat*. We also specialize in gift books for children on the occasions of Baptism and First Communion, as well as other important times in a child's life, and books that bring creativity and liveliness to any adult spiritual life.

The MOUNT TABOR BOOKS series focuses on the arts and literature as well as liturgical worship and spirituality; it was created in conjunction with the Mount Tabor Ecumenical Centre for Art and Spirituality in Barga, Italy.

Music

PARACLETE PRESS DISTRIBUTES RECORDINGS of the internationally acclaimed choir *Gloriæ Dei Cantores*, the *Gloriæ Dei Cantores Schola*, and the other instrumental artists of the *Arts Empowering Life Foundation*.

PARACLETE PRESS IS THE EXCLUSIVE NORTH AMERICAN DISTRIBUTOR for the Gregorian chant recordings from St. Peter's Abbey in Solesmes, France. Paraclete also carries all of the Solesmes chant publications for Mass and the Divine Office, as well as their academic research publications.

In addition, PARACLETE PRESS SHEET MUSIC publishes the work of today's finest composers of sacred choral music, annually reviewing over 1,000 works and releasing between 40 and 60 works for both choir and organ.

Video

Our video/DVDs offer spiritual help, healing, and biblical guidance for a broad range of life issues including grief and loss, marriage, forgiveness, facing death, understanding suicide, bullying, addictions, Alzheimer's, and Christian formation.

Learn more about us at our website:
www.paracletepress.com
or phone us toll-free at 1.800.451.5006

SCAN
TO
READ

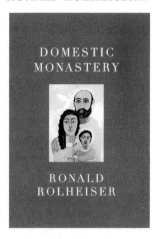

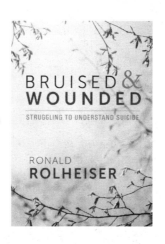

Bruised and Wounded
Struggling to Understand Suicide
ISBN 978-1-64060-084-3 | Trade paperback | $12.99

"Ron Rolheiser takes on the difficult issue of suicide
in his usual style, writing with both compassion and
empathy. This book offers hope and healing to those who
have experienced the loss of a loved one or
anyone trying to understand the topic."

—Catholic News Service

Available at bookstores

Paraclete Press | 1-800-451-5006 | www.paracletepress.com